Rebound 1982

THE COMPLETE ETCHINGS OF

Goya

THE COMPLETE ETCHINGS OF

With a Foreword by Aldous Huxley

CROWN PUBLISHERS · NEW YORK

Contents

Publisher's Note: Throughout this book the Spanish captions of the etchings, given to them by Goya, will be found together with English translations. In a few instances no Spanish titles are known. In such cases the accepted French captions, from the definitive catalogue by Loys Delteil, are given.

Foreword

BY ALDOUS HUXLEY

T HERE ARE anthologies of almost everything—from the best to the worst, from the historically significant to the eccentric, from the childish to the sublime. But there is one anthology, potentially the most interesting of them all, which, to the best of my knowledge, has never yet been compiled; I mean, the Anthology of Later Works.

To qualify for inclusion in such an anthology, the artist would have to pass several tests. First of all, he must have avoided a premature extinction and lived on into artistic and chronological maturity. Thus the last poems of Shelley, the last compositions of Schubert and even of Mozart would find no place in our collection. Consummate artists as they were, these men were still psychologically youthful when they died. For their full development they needed more time than their earthly destiny allowed them. Of a different order are those strange beings whose chronological age is out of all proportion to their maturity, not only as artists, but as human spirits. Thus, some of the letters written by Keats in his early twenties and many of the paintings which Seurat executed before his death at thirty-two might certainly qualify as Later Works. But, as a general rule, a certain minimum of time is needed for the ripening of such fruits. For the most part, our hypothetical anthologist will make his selections from the art of elderly and middle-aged men and women.

But by no means all middle-aged and elderly artists are capable of producing significant Later Works. For the last half century of a long life, Wordsworth preserved an almost unbroken record of dulness. And in this respect he does not stand alone. There are many, many others whose Later Works are their worst. All these must be excluded from our anthology, and I would pass a similar judgment on that other large class of Later Works, which, though up to the standard of the earlier, are not significantly different from them. Haydn lived to a ripe old age and his right hand never forgot its cunning; but it also failed to learn a new cunning. Peter Pan-like, he continued, as an old man, to write the same sort of thing he had written twenty, thirty and forty years before. Where there is nothing to distinguish the creations of a man's maturity from those of his youth it is superfluous to include any of them in a selection of characteristically Later Works.

This leaves us, then, with the Later Works of those artists who have lived without ever ceasing to learn of life. The field is relatively narrow; but within it, what astonishing, and sometimes what disquieting treasures! One thinks of the ineffable serenity of the slow movement of Beethoven's *A minor quartet*, the peace passing all understanding of the orchestral prelude to the *Benedictus* of his *Missa Solemnis*. But this is not the old man's only mood; when he turns from the contemplation of eternal reality to a consideration of the human world, we are treated to the positively terrifying merriment of the *Scherzo* in his *B flat major quartet*—merriment quite inhuman, peals of violent and yet somehow abstract laughter echoing down from somewhere beyond the limits of the world. Of the same nature, but if possible even more disquieting, is the mirth which reverberates through the last act of Verdi's *Falstaff*, culminating in that extraordinary final chorus in which the aged genius makes his maturest comment on the world—not with bitterness or sarcasm or satire, but in a huge, contrapuntal paroxysm of detached and already posthumous laughter. A similar detachment—but not associated with laughter and therefore less hair-raising than the detachment of *Falstaff* or the *B flat major scherzo*—is the characteristic feature of Bach's *Art of the Fugue*.

Turning to the other arts, we find something of the same non-human, posthumous quality in the Later Works of Yeats and, coupled with a prodigious majesty, in those of Piero della Francesca. And then, of course there is *The Tempest*—a work charged with something of the unearthly serenity of Beethoven's *Benedictus* but concluding in the most disappointing anti-climax, with Prospero giving up his magic for the sake (heaven help us!) of becoming once again a duke. And the same sort of all too human anti-climax saddens us at the end of the second part of *Faust*, with its implication that draining fens is Man's Final End, and that the achievement of this end automatically qualifies the drainer for the beatific vision. Still, in spite of those touches of what every exponent of the Perennial Philosophy would put down as spiritual immaturity, both of them remain Later Works on the grand scale.

And what about the last El Grecos—for example, that unimaginable *Assumption* at Toledo with its fantastic harmony of brilliant, ice-cold colors, its ecstatic gesticulations in a heaven with a third dimension no greater than that of a mine-shaft, its deliquescence of flesh and flowers and drapery into a set of ectoplasmic abstractions? What about them, indeed? All we know is that, beautiful and supremely enigmatic, they will certainly take their place in our hypothetical anthology.

And finally, among these and all other extraordinary Later Works, we should have to number the paintings, drawings and etchings of Goya's final twenty-five or thirty years.

The difference between the young Goya and the old may be best studied and appreciated by starting in the basement of the Prado, where his cartoons for the tapestries are hung; climbing thence to the main floor, where there is a room full of his portraits of royal imbeciles, grandees, enchanting duchesses, *majas*, clothed and unclothed; walking thence to the smaller room containing the two great paintings of the Second of May—Napoleon's Mamelukes cutting down the crowd and, at night, when the revolt has been quelled, the firing squads at work upon their victims by the light of lanterns; and finally mounting to the top floor where hang the etchings and drawings, together with those unutterably mysterious and disturbing "black paintings," with which the deaf and aging Goya elected to adorn the dining-room of his house, the *Quinta del Sordo*. It is a progress from light-hearted eighteenth-century art, hardly at all unconventional in subject matter or in handling, through fashionable brilliancy and increasing virtuosity to something quite timeless both in technique and spirit—the most powerful of commentaries on human crime and madness, made in terms of an artistic convention uniquely fitted to express precisely that extraordinary mingling of hatred and compassion, despair and sardonic humor, realism and fantasy.

"I show you sorrow," said the Buddha, "and the ending of sorrow"—the sorrow of the phenomenal world in which man, "like an angry ape, plays such fantastic tricks before high heaven as make the angels weep," and the ending of sorrow in the beatific vision, the unitive contemplation of transcendental reality. Apart from the fact that he is a great and one might say, uniquely original artist, Goya is significant as being, in his Later Works, the almost perfect type of the man who knows only sorrow and not the ending of sorrow—who can give expression to the equivalent only of *Falstaff*, not of the *Requiem*, only of the *B flat major scherzo*, not of the *Benedictus*.

In spite of his virulent anti-clericalism, Goya contrived to remain on sufficiently good terms with the Church to receive periodical commissions to paint religious pictures. Some of these, like the frescoes in the cupola of La Florida, are frankly and avowedly secular. But others are serious essays in religious painting. It is worth looking rather closely at what is probably the best of these religious pieces—the fine *Agony in the Garden*. With outstretched arms, Christ raises towards the comforting angel a face whose expression is identical with that of the poor creatures whom we see, in a number of unforgettably painful etchings and paintings, kneeling or standing in an excruciating anticipation before the gun barrels of a French firing squad. There is no trace here of that loving confidence which, even in the darkest hours, fills the hearts of men and women who live continually in the presence of God; not so much as a hint of what Francois de Sales calls "holy indifference" to suffering and good fortune, of the fundamental equanimity, the peace passing all understanding which belongs to those whose attention is firmly fixed upon a transcendental reality.

For Goya the transcendental reality did not exist. There is no evidence in his biography or his works that he ever had even the most distant personal experience of it. The only reality he knew was that of the world around him; and the longer he lived the more frightful did that world seem—the more frightful, that is to say, in the eyes of his rational self; for his animal high spirits went on bubbling up irrepressibly, whenever his body was free from pain or sickness, to the very end. As a young man in good health, with money and reputation, a fine position and as many women as he wanted, he had found the world a very agreeable place. Absurd, of course, and with enough of folly and roguery to furnish subject matter for innumerable satirical drawings, but eminently worth living in. Then all of a sudden came deafness; and, after the joyful dawn of the Revolution, Napoleon and French Imperialism and the atrocities of war; and, when Napoleon's hordes were gone, the unspeakable Ferdinand VII and clerical reaction and the spectacle of Spaniards fighting among themselves; and all the time, like the drone of a bagpipe accompanying the louder noises of what is officially called history, the enormous stupidity of average men and women, the chronic squalor of their superstitions, the bestiality of their occasional violences and orgies.

Realistically or in fantastic allegories, with a technical mastery that only increased as he grew older, Goya recorded it all. Not only the agonies endured by his people at the hands of the invaders, but also the follies and crimes committed by these same people in their dealings with one another. The great canvases of the Madrid massacres and executions, the incomparable etchings of War's Disasters, fill us with an indignant compassion. But then we turn to the *Disparates* and the *Pinturas Negras*. In these, with a sublimely impartial savagery, Goya sets down exactly what he thinks of the martyrs of the *Dos de Mayo*, when they are not being martyred. Here, for example, are two men—two Spaniards—sinking slowly towards death in an engulfing quicksand, but busily engaged in knocking one another over the head with bludgeons. And here is a rabble coming home from a pilgrimage—scores of low faces, distorted as though by reflection in the back of a spoon, all open-mouthed and yelling. And all the blank black eyes stare vacantly and idiotically in different directions.

These creatures who haunt Goya's Later Works are inexpressibly horrible, with the horror of mindlessness and animality and spiritual darkness. And above the lower depths where they obscenely pullulate is a world of bad priests and lustful friars, of fascinating women whose love is a "dream of lies and inconsistency," of fatuous nobles and, at the top of the social pyramid, a royal family of half-wits, sadists, Messalinas and perjurers. The moral of it all is summed up in the central plate of the *Caprichos*, in which we see Goya himself, his head on his arms, sprawled across his desk and fitfully sleeping, while the air above is peopled with the bats and owls of necromancy and just behind his chair lies an enormous witch's cat, malevolent as only Goya's cats can be, staring at the sleeper with baleful eyes. On the side of the desk are traced the words, "The dream of reason produces monsters." It is a caption that admits of more than one interpretation. When reason sleeps, the absurd and loathsome creatures of superstition wake and are active, goading their victim to an ignoble frenzy. But this is not all, Reason may also dream without sleeping; may intoxicate itself, as it did during the French Revolution, with the day-dreams of inevitable progress, of liberty, equality and fraternity imposed by violence, of human self-sufficiency and the ending of sorrow, not by the all too arduous method which alone offers any prospect of success, but by political re-arrangements and a better technology. The *Caprichos* were published in the last year of the eighteenth century; in 1808 Goya and all Spain were given the opportunity of discovering the consequences of such day-dreaming. Murat marched his troops into Madrid; the *Desastres de la Guerra* were about to begin.

Goya produced four main sets of etchings—the *Caprichos*, the *Desastres de la Guerra*, the *Tauromaquia* and the *Disparates* or *Proverbios*. All of them are Later Works. The *Caprichos* were not published until he was fifty-three; the plates of the *Desastres* were etched between the ages of sixty-five and seventy-five; the *Tauromaquia* series first saw the light when he was sixty-nine (and at the age of almost eighty he learnt the brand new technique of lithography in order to be able to do justice to his beloved bulls in yet another medium); the *Disparates* were finished when he was seventy-three.

For the non-Spaniard the plates of the *Tauromaquia* series will probably seem the least interesting of Goya's etchings. They are brilliant records of the exploits of the bull ring; but unfortunately, or fortunately, most of us know very little about bullfighting. Consequently, we miss the finer shades of the significance of these little masterpieces of documentary art. Moreover, being documentary, the etchings of the *Tauromaquia* do not lend themselves to being executed with that splendid audacity, that dramatic breadth of treatment, which delight us in the later paintings and the etchings of the other three series. True, we find in this collection a few plates that are as fine as anything Goya ever produced—for example, that wonderful etching of the bull which has broken out of the arena and stands triumphant, a corpse hanging limp across its horns, among the spectators' benches. But by and large it is not to the *Tauromaquia* that we turn for the very best specimens of Goya's work in black and white, or for the most characteristic expressions of his mature personality. The nature of the subject matter makes it impossible for him, in these plates, to reveal himself fully either as a man or as an artist.

Of the three other sets of etchings two, the *Caprichos* and *Disparates*, are fantastic and allegorical in subject matter, while the third, the *Desastres*, though for the most part it represents real happenings under the Napoleonic terror, represents them in a way which, being generalized and symbolical, rather than directly documentary, permits of, and indeed demands, a treatment no less broad and dramatic than is given to the fantasies of the other collections.

War always weakens and often completely shatters the crust of customary decency which constitutes a civilization. It is a thin crust at the best of times, and beneath it lies— what? Look through Goya's *Desastres* and find out. The abyss of bestiality and diabolism and suffering seems almost bottomless. There is practically nothing of which human be- ings are not capable when war or revolution or anarchy gives them the necessary oppor- tunity and excuse; and to their pain death alone imposes a limit.

Goya's record of disaster has a number of recurrent themes. There are those shadowy archways, for example, more sinister than those even of Piranesi's Prisons, where women are violated, captives squat in a hopeless stupor, corpses lie rotting, emaciated children starve to death. Then there are the vague street corners at which the famine-stricken hold out their hands; but the whiskered French hussars and carabiniers look on without pity, and even the rich Spaniards pass by indifferently, as though they were "of another lineage." Of still more frequent occurrence in the series are the crests of those naked hillocks on which lie the dead, like so much garbage. Or else, in dramatic silhouette against the sky above those same hilltops, we see the hideous butchery of Spanish men and women, and the no less hideous vengeance meted out by infuriated Spaniards upon their tormentors. Often the hillock sprouts a single tree, always low, sometimes maimed by gun-fire. Upon its branches are impaled, like the beetles and caterpillars in a butcher bird's larder, whole naked torsos, sometimes decapitated, sometimes without arms; or else a pair of amputated legs, or a severed head—warnings, set there by the conquerors, of the fate awaiting those who dare oppose the Emperor. At other times the tree is used as a gallows—a less efficient gallows, indeed, than that majestic oak which, in Callot's *Misères de la Guerre*, is fruited with more than a score of swinging corpses, but good enough for a couple of executions *en passant*, except, of course, in the case recorded in one of Goya's most hair-raising plates, in which the tree is too stumpy to permit of a man's hanging clear of the ground. But the rope is fixed, none the less, and to tighten the noose around their victim's neck, two French soldiers tug at the legs, while with his foot a third man thrusts with all his strength against the shoulders.

And so the record proceeds, horror after horror, unalleviated by any of the splendors which other painters have been able to discover in war; for, significantly, Goya never illustrates an engagement, never shows us impressive masses of troops marching in column or deployed in the order of battle. His concern is exclusively with war as it affects the civilian population, with armies disintegrated into individual thieves and ravishers, tormentors and executioners—and occasionally, when the *guerilleros* have won a skirmish, into individual victims tortured in their turn and savagely done to death by the avengers of their own earlier atrocities. All he shows us is war's disasters and squalors, without any of the glory or even picturesqueness.

In the two remaining series of etchings we pass from tragedy to satire and from historical fact to allegory and pictorial metaphor and pure fantasy. Twenty years separate the *Caprichos* from the *Disparates*, and the later collection is at once more sombre and more enigmatic than the earlier. Much of the satire of the *Caprichos* is merely Goya's sharper version of what may be called standard eighteenth-century humor. A plate such as *Hasta la Muerte*, showing the old hag before her mirror, coquettishly trying on a new head-dress, is just Rowlandson-with-a-difference. But in certain other etchings a stranger and more disquieting note is struck. Goya's handling of his material is such that standard eighteenth-century humor often undergoes a sea-change into something darker and queerer, something that goes below the anecdotal surface of life into what lies beneath —the unplumbed depths of original sin and original stupidity. And in the second half of the series the subject matter reinforces the effect of the powerful and dramatically sinister treatment; for here the theme of almost all the plates is basely supernatural. We are in a world of demons, witches and familiars, half horrible, half comic, but wholly disquieting inasmuch as it reveals the sort of thing that goes on in the squalid catacombs of the human mind.

In the *Disparates* the satire is on the whole less direct than in the *Caprichos*, the allegories are more general and more mysterious. Consider, for example, the technically astonishing plate, which shows a large family of three generations perched like huddling birds along a huge dead branch that projects into the utter vacancy of a dark sky. Obviously, much more is meant than meets the eye. But what? The question is one upon which the commentators have spent a great deal of ingenuity—spent it, one may suspect, in vain. For the satire, it would seem, is not directed against this particular social evil or that political mistake, but rather against unregenerate human nature as such. It is a statement, in the form of an image, about life in general. Literature and the scriptures of all the great religions abound in such brief metaphorical verdicts on human destiny. Man, turns the wheel of sorrow, burns in the fire of craving, travels through a vale of tears, leads a life that is no better than a tale told by an idiot signifying nothing.

Poor man, what art? A tennis ball of error,
A ship of glass tossed in a sea of terror:
Issuing in blood and sorrow from the womb,
Crawling in tears and mourning to the tomb.
How slippery are thy paths, how sure thy fall!
How art thou nothing, when thou art most of all!

And so on. Good, bad and indifferent, the quotations could be multiplied almost indefinitely. In the language of the plastic arts, Goya has added a score of memorable contributions to the stock of humanity's gnomic wisdom.

The *Disparate* of the dead branch is relatively easy to understand. So is the comment on Fear contained in the plate which shows soldiers running in terror from a gigantic cowled figure, spectral against a jet black sky. So is the etching of the ecstatically smiling woman riding a stallion that turns its head and, seizing her skirts between its teeth, tries to drag her from her seat. The allegorical use of the horse, as a symbol of the senses and the passions, and of the rational rider or charioteer who is at liberty to direct or be run away with, is at least as old as Plato.

But there are other plates in which the symbolism is less clear, the allegorical significance far from obvious. That horse on a tight-rope, for example, with a woman dancing on its back; the men who fly with artificial wings against a sky of inky menace; the priests and the elephant; the old man wandering among phantoms. What is the meaning of these things? And perhaps the answer to that question is that they have no meaning in any ordinary sense of the word; that they refer to strictly private events taking place on the obscurer levels of their creator's mind. For us who look at them, it may be that their real point and significance consist precisely in the fact that they image forth so vividly and yet, of necessity, so darkly and incomprehensibly, some at least of the unknown quantities that exist at the heart of every personality.

Goya once drew a picture of an ancient man tottering along under the burden of years, but with the accompanying caption, "I'm still learning." That old man was himself. To the end of a long life, he went on learning. As a very young man he paints like the feeble eclectics who were his masters. The first signs of power and freshness and originality appear in the cartoons for the tapestries of which the earliest were executed when he was thirty. As a portraitist, however, he achieves nothing of outstanding interest until he is almost forty. But by that time he really knows what he's after, and during the second forty years of his life he moves steadily forward towards the consummate technical achievements, in oils, of the *Pinturas Negras*, and, in etching, of the *Desastres* and the *Disparates*. Goya's is a stylistic growth away from restraint and into freedom, away from timidity and into expressive boldness.

From the technical point of view the most striking fact about almost all Goya's successful paintings and etchings is that they are composed in terms of one or more clearly delimited masses standing out from the background, often indeed, silhouetted against the sky. When he attempts what may be called an "all-over" composition, the essay is rarely successful. For he lacks almost completely the power which Rubens so conspicuously possessed—of filling the entire canvas with figures or details of landscape, and upon that *plenum* imposing a clear and yet exquisitely subtle three-dimensional order. The lack of this power is already conspicuous in the tapestry cartoons, of which the best are invariably those in which Goya does his composing in terms of silhouetted masses and the worst those in which he attempts to organize a collection of figures distributed all over the canvas. And compare, from this point of view, the two paintings of the *Dos de Mayo*—the Mamelukes cutting down the crowd in the Puerta del Sol, and the firing squads at work in the suburbs, after dark. The first is an attempt to do what Rubens would have done with an almost excessive facility—to impose a formally beautiful and dramatically significant order upon a crowd of human and animal figures covering the greater part of the canvas. The attempt is not successful, and in spite of its power and the beauty of its component parts, the picture as a whole is less satisfying as a composition, and for that reason less moving as a story, than is the companion piece, in which Goya arranges his figures in a series of sharply delimited balancing groups, dramatically contrasted with one another and the background. In this picture the artist is speaking his native language, and he is therefore able to express what he wants to say with the maximum force and clarity. This is not the case with the picture of the Mamelukes. Here, the formal language is not truly his own, and consequently his eloquence lacks the moving power it possesses when he lets himself go in the genuine Goyescan idiom.

Fortunately, in the etchings, Goya is very seldom tempted to talk in anything else. Here he composes almost exclusively in terms of bold separate masses, silhouetted in luminous grays and whites against a darkness that ranges from stippled pepper-and-salt to intense black, or in blacks and heavily shaded grays against the whiteness of virgin paper. Sometimes there is only one mass, sometimes several, balanced and contrasted. Hardly ever does he make the, for him, almost fatal mistake of trying to organize his material in an all-over composition.

With the *Desastres* and the *Disparates* his mastery of this, his predestined method of composition becomes, one might say, absolute. It is not, of course, the only method of composition. Indeed, the nature of this particular artistic idiom is such that there are probably certain things that can never be expressed in it—things which Rembrandt, for example, was able to say in his supremely beautiful and subtle illustrations to the Bible. But within the field that he chose to cultivate—that the idiosyncrasies of his temperament and the quality of his artistic sensibilities compelled him to choose—Goya remains incomparable.

The Capriccios

(LOS CAPRICHOS)

In addition to the Spanish and translated captions of the *Capriccios*, from the plates themselves, Goya's commentaries on the etchings are also given. The manuscript of these is now in the Prado. The authentic numbers for the series are on the upper right corners of the plates.

22 POOR LITTLE THINGS!—*Pobrecitas!*
They will have to repair what has long been going from bad to worse, to fix what has been forced apart.

23 SEE THE RESULT—*Aquellos polbos*
From such dust such dirt must come. For shame, to treat her in such fashion! She who has waited on everyone for a trifle, she who was so industrious, so useful; she was an honorable woman.

24 THERE WAS NO CURE—*Nohubo remedio*
They have made up their minds to kill this good woman. After judgment was pronounced, she was dragged through the streets in triumph. She has indeed earned a triumph. If they do this to shame her, they are wasting their time. Nothing can make her ashamed who has nothing to be ashamed of.

25 THE PITCHER BROKE—*Si quebró el Cantaro*
The boy is a scamp, and the mother is a nag. What a pair!

26 PLENTY OF ROOM—*Ya tienen asiento*
These nice girls have enough chairs, but they know nothing better to do with them than to wear them on their heads.

27 WHICH OF THE TWO LOVES MORE?—*Quien mas rendido?*
Neither cares for the other. He pretends to love and says the same thing to every woman he meets. She is wondering how to keep her five dates between eight and nine—and it is seven-thirty now.

28 HUSH-SH-SH—*Chiton*
An excellent woman to trust with a confidential message.

29 THEY CALL THIS READING—*Esto si que es leer*
He is having his hair combed, his stockings drawn on, his sleep and his studies at the same time. No one can say he is not making the most of time.

30 WHY HIDE THE MONEY?—*Porque esconderlos?*
The answer is easy. He won't spend it; he doesn't spend it; he can't spend it. Although he is over eighty and has barely another month to live, he is afraid that he might have no more left if he lives longer. Such are the mistakes of greed.

31 SHE PRAYS FOR HER—*Ruega por ella*
And she did well to do so . . . that God may give her luck, keep her from harm, moneylenders, and cops . . . make her skilful and careful, wide-awake, and ready as her sainted mother.

32 SHE WAS SO EASILY INFLUENCED—*Por que fue sensible*
This was to be expected. The world has its ups and downs and the life she led has no other end.

33 TO THE COUNT PALATINE—*Al Conde Palatino*
In all sciences there are people who know everything without having learned and have a ready remedy for all ills. One can't believe what they say. The really intelligent person mistrusts them. The educated person makes moderate promises and keeps much in reserve. The Count Palatine never keeps any promises at all.

34 THEY ARE ASLEEP—*Las rinde el Sueño*
Don't wake them. Sleep is the only happiness of the miserable.

35 SHE KNOWS HOW TO PLUCK HER GOOSE—*Le descañona*
They strip him to the skin. It is his own fault for trusting such.

36 A STORMY NIGHT—*Mala noche*
These are the dangers which streetwalkers face.

37 CAN THE PUPIL KNOW MORE?—*Si sabrà mas el discipulo?*
It's hard to say, but the teacher is trying his best.

38 BRAVISSIMO!—*Brabisimo!*
If the size of the ears makes a good listener, he should know a lot. Most likely, he is applauding not knowing what.

39 AS FAR BACK AS HIS GRANDFATHER—*Asta su Abuelo*
This poor wretch is driven mad by genealogy and heraldry. He isn't the only one.

40 OF WHAT WILL HE DIE?—*De que mal morira?*
The doctor is doing his best. What more can we expect?

41 NEITHER MORE NOR LESS—*Ni mas ni menos*
Lucky he had his portrait painted. Now they who have not seen him will know what he was like.

42 THEY CANNOT HELP IT—*Tu que no puedes*
You can't deny that these two cavaliers—are cavalry men. (An untranslatable pun.)

43 THE DREAM OF REASON PRODUCES MONSTERS—*El sueño de la razon produce monstruos*
Imagination deserted by reason creates impossible, useless thoughts. United with reason, imagination is the mother of all art and the source of all its beauty.

44 THEY SPIN—*Hilan delgado*
So finely do they spin that the devil himself will not be able to tear the cloth they are weaving.

45 THERE IS A LOT TO SUCK—*Mucho hay que chupar*
At eighty they suck little children dry; they who do not live more than eighteen, suck big children. It looks as if man is born into this world and lives just to have the marrow sucked out of him.

46 CORRECTIONS—*Correccion*
Without punishment and self-discipline one can't get on in any science. In witchcraft one needs unusual talent, perseverance, maturity, and a rigid obedience to the teachings of the Great Witchmaster who conducts the Seminary of Barahona.

47 HOMAGE TO THE MASTER—*Obsequio á el maestro*
This is only natural. They would be ungrateful students not to entertain their teacher who taught them all they know about the dark sciences.

48 THE BLOWERS—*Soplones*
The blowing witches are the most revolting and most stupid in the devil's league. If they had any sense they would not blow.

49 LITTLE DEVILS—*Duendecitos*
Quite a different kind of people! Jolly, quick, useful—perhaps a bit selfish, somewhat prone to play childish tricks—but very nice, very good-natured little fellows.

50 THE CHINCHILLA RATS—*Los Chinchillas*
People who will not listen, people who are ignorant and never do anything useful, belong to the family of the Chinchilla rats. They are good for nothing.

51 THEY PARE THEIR OWN NAILS—*Se repulen*
Long nails are so nasty and dirty a habit that it is even forbidden among the witches.

52 FINE FEATHERS MAKE FINE BIRDS!—*Lo que puede un Sastre!*
Often an idiot, a mere nobody, is gotten up to look like somebody. This is the result of the tailor's art and the blindness of most people who judge only by the outside.

53 WHAT A GOLDEN BEAK!—*Que pico de Oro!*
This is an academic session. Is the parrot speaking on some medical subject? Don't you believe what he says. There is many a doctor who has the golden beak when he is talking but is useless when it comes to prescribing. He can describe diseases in the most able manner, but he can't cure them. He beguiles the sick and fills the churchyard with skulls.

54 THE PIMP (PANDER)—*El Vergonzoso*
There are people whose faces are the most shameful part of their bodies. It would be a good thing if those who have such obscene faces were to hide them in their pants. How shameful!

55 TILL DEATH—*Hasta la muerte*
She is right to doll herself up. It is her birthday. She is 75 years old and her friends are coming to see her.

56 UPS AND DOWNS—*Subir y bajar*
Fortune is unkind to those who court her. Ambition is rewarded with emptiness. Those who have risen she often punishes with downfall.

57 THE BETROTHAL—*La filiacion*
See them overcome the bridegroom by showing him who the parents, grandparents, great-grandparents, and great-great-grandparents of the young lady were; but who is she? He will find this out later.

58 EAT THAT, YOU DOG—*Tragala, perro*
Living among people is full of annoyances. Whoever wants to avoid them should go into the wilderness. There he will find that loneliness is a greater annoyance.

59 THEY'RE THERE!—*Y aun no se van!*
He who is indifferent to the favors of fortune sleeps calmly through all danger. Nevertheless, danger threatens him and he cannot avoid the misfortunes that will befall him.

60 TRIALS—*Ensayos*
Gradually he makes progress. Now he can jump a little. In time he will do even as much as his teacher.

61 VOLAVERUNT—*Volaverunt*
The witches which serve as a pedestal to this fashion's fool are more ornamental than useful. There are heads so swelled with hot air that they need neither broom nor witches to make them fly.

62 WHO WOULD BELIEVE IT!—*Quien lo creyera!*
See them fight as to which is the bigger witch. Who would have believed that they would tear each other to pieces in such an insane fashion. Friendship is a virtue. Criminals may be accomplices but never friends.

63 LOOK, ARE WE NOT WONDERFUL!—*Miren que grabes!*
See two nice and highly respected witches out for a ride.

64 BON VOYAGE—*Buen Viage*
Where is this hellish company going to, filling the darkness of night with their shrieks? If it were day it would be different; the whole crew would be brought down by guns. It is night. No one can see them.

65 WHERE IS MAMA GOING?—*Donde vá mamà?*
Mother is sick and is going out for a walk. God grant that she may recover!

66 THERE THEY GO—*Allá vá eso*
The witch is riding on a crippled devil. This poor devil whom everyone scorns is sometimes very useful.

67 WAIT UNTIL YOU HAVE BEEN PROPERLY ANOINTED —*Aguarda que te unten*
He's been given an important errand but wants to go off half anointed. Even among witches there are thoughtless, foolish, imprudent members. It is the same everywhere.

68 PRETTY TEACHER!—*Linda maestra!*
The broom is perhaps the most essential tool for a witch. For besides being useful for sweeping, it can, according to many a story, be changed into a mule that runs so fast that even the devil himself can't catch up with it.

69 SHE BLOWS—*Sopla*
Surely, there was a great catch of children yesterday. The banquet being prepared will be a large one. Hearty appetite!

70 VOWS—*Devota profesion*
Do you swear to obey your masters or those in authority . . . to honor them, to sweep, to spin, to beat drums, to howl, to yell, to fly, to cook, to suck, to bake, to roast, and everything else whenever you are ordered? . . . I swear . . . Very well, you are a witch, my dear. Congratulations!

71 THE DAY IS BREAKING, AWAY—*Si amanece; nos Vamos*
If you didn't come, you won't have been missed.

72 YOU CANNOT ESCAPE—*No te escaparàs*
No one ever escapes who wants to be caught.

73 IT IS BETTER TO DO NOTHING—*Mejor es holgar*
He who does not enjoy his work is quite right in saying, "It is better to do nothing."

74 DON'T CRY, IDIOT—*No grites, tonta*
Poor little Frances. She went out to see the footman but met the goblin. Don't be afraid! The goblin is in good temper and he won't do you any harm.

75 WILL NO ONE SET US FREE?—*No hay quien nos desate?*
A man and a woman are tied together. They are trying with all their might to free themselves and are calling for help. If

I'm not mistaken, they are two people who were forced to marry.

76 YOUR EXCELLENCY IS . . . H-M-M . . . AS I WAS SAYING . . . YES. H-M-M . . . BE CAREFUL!—*Esta Vm^d pues, Como digo . . . eh! Cuidado! si nó . . .*
The uniform, sign of the dignity of a commander, and the baton of command, makes this blockhead imagine himself a superior being. He misuses his office to annoy everyone who knows him. He is proud, vain, insolent to his inferiors in rank, cringing to all above him.

77 NOW ONE, NOW ANOTHER—*Unos à otros*
The way of the world. The people laugh and play bullfighting with each other. He who yesterday played the bull plays today the toreador. Chance rules the game and assigns the parts according to her caprices.

78 HURRY, THEY'RE WAKING UP—*Despacha, que dispiertan*
The brownies are a most industrious and helpful little people. The housemaid is very friendly towards them so they clean her pots, cook the vegetables, dust and sweep, and take care of the baby for her. People argue whether they are devils or not. That is quite useless. Devils are those who are busy causing trouble and hindering others from doing good—or, *they do nothing at all.*

79 NOBODY SAW US—*Nadie nos ha visto*
What does it matter if the brownies go down the wine cellar to have an occasional glass after they have worked all night polishing the cask's tap so that it shines and glows like bright gold?

80 'TIS THE HOUR. TIME TO BE OFF—*Ya es hora*
When dawn breaks they fly away . . . each to his place. The witches, the hobgoblins, the dreams, the phantoms. It is lucky that such creatures only show themselves by night in the dark. No one has yet discovered where they hide in the daytime. If one were to succeed in trapping some goblins and showing them in a cage on the Puerta del Sol, it would make him his fortune.

Fran.^{co} Goya y Lucientes,
Pintor.

El si pronuncian y la mano alargan
Al primero que llega.

Que viene el Coco.

El de la rollona

Tal para qual.

17734

Nadie se conoce.

Ni asi la distingue.

Que se la llevaron!

Tantalo.

El amor y la muerte.

Muchachos al avío.

A caza de dientes.

Estan calientes.

Que sacrificio!

Bellos consejos.

Dios la perdone: Y era su madre.

Bien tirada está.

Ysele quema la Casa.

Todos Caerán.

Ya van desplumados.

¡Qual la descañonan!

Pobrecitas!

Aquellos polbos.

Nohubo remedio.

Si quebró el Cantaro.

Ya tienen asiento.

Quien mas rendido?

Chiton.

Esto si que es leer.

Porque esconderlos?

Ruega por ella.

Por que fue sensible.

Al Conde Palatino.

Las rinde el Sueño.

Le descañona.

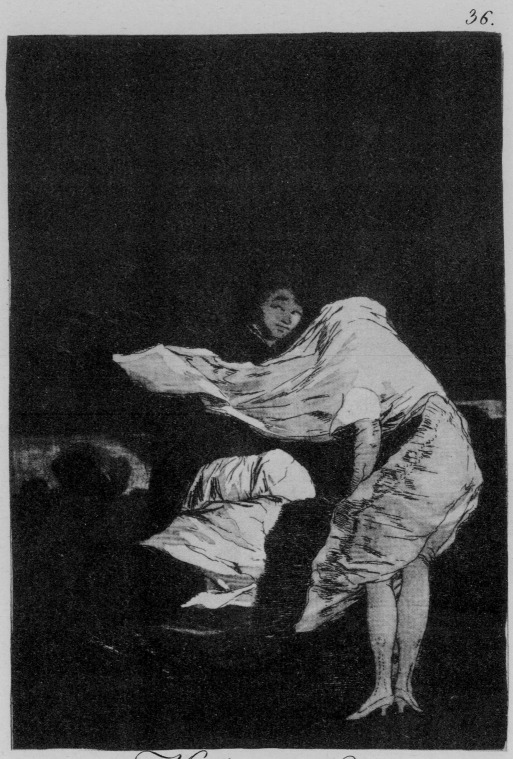

Mala noche.

Si sabrà mas el discipulo?

Brabisimo!

Asta su Abuelo.

De que mal morira?

Ni mas ni menos.

Tu que no puedes.

Hilan delgado.

Mucho hay que chupar.

Correccion.

Obsequio á el maestro.

Soplones.

Duendecitos.

Los Chinchillas.

Se repulen.

Lo que puede un Sastre!

Que pico de Oro!

El Vergonzoso.

Hasta la muerte.

Subir y bajar.

La filiacion.

Tragala perro.

Y aun no se van!

Ensayos.

Volaverunt.

Quien lo creyera!

Miren que grabes!

Buen Viage

Donde vá mamá!

Allá vá eso.

Aguarda que te unten.

Linda maestra!

Sopla.

Devota profesion.

Si amanece ; nos Vamos.

No te escaparás.

Mejor es holgar.

No grites, tonta.

¿No hay quien nos desate?

¿Està Vm.ᵈ pues, Como digo.. eh'Cuidado'si nó..

Unos á otros.

Despacha, que dispiërtan.

Nadie nos ha visto.

Ya es hora.

The Disasters of the War

(LOS DESASTRES DE LA GUERRA)

The authentic numbers of this series are found at the upper left corners of the plates. Numbers 81, 82, and 83 are plates discovered after the issuing of the early editions. They are rare and are not available in the United States. For this reason they are reproduced in small size from other reproductions.

Tristes presentimientos de lo que ha de acontecer.

Con razon ó sin ella.

Lo mismo.

3

4

Las mugeres dan valor.

5

Y son fieras

Bien te se está.

Que valor!

Siempre sucede.

No quieren.

Tampoco

10

11

Ni por esas.

12

Para eso habeis nacido.

13

Amarga presencia.

14

¡Duro es el paso!

Y no hai remedio.

15

Se aprovechan.

17

No se convienen.

18

Enterrar y callar.

Ya no hay tiempo.

20.

Curarlos, y a otra

Será lo mismo

Tanto y mas

23

Lo mismo en otras partes

24

Aun podrán servir

25

Tambien estos.

No se puede mirar

27

Goya 1810

Caridad.

28

Populacho.

Lo merecia.

30

Estragos de la guerra

Fuerte cosa es!

32

Por qué?

Qué hai que hacer mas?

33

34

Por una navaja.

35.

No se puede saber por qué.

36

Tampoco.

37

Esto es peor.

Bárbaros!

39

Grande hazaña! Con muertos!

40.

Alyun partido saca.

41

Escapan entre las llamas.

Todo va revuelto.

43

Tambien esto.

44

Yo lo vi.

45

Y esto tambien.

46

Esto es malo.

Asi sucedió.

47

48

Cruel lástima!

49

Caridad de una muger.

50.

Madre infeliz!

61

Gracias á la almorta.

52

No llegan á tiempo.

58

Espiró sin remedio.

54

Clamores en vano.

55

Lo peor es pedir

Al cementerio

51

Sanos y enfermos.

No hay que dar voces.

59

De qué sirve una taza?

6.

No hay quien los socorra.

Si son de otro linage.

62

Las camas de la muerte.

63

Muertos recogidos.

64

Carretadas al cementerio.

65

Qué alboroto es este?

Extraña devocion!

Esta no lo es menos.

67

68

Que locura!

Nada. Ello dirá.

10

No saben el camino.

Contra el bien general.

72

Las resultas.

73

Gatesca pantomima.

14

Esto es lo peor!

75

Farándula de charlatanes.

El buitre carnívoro.

77

Que se rompe la cuerda.

18

Se defiende bien.

Murió la Verdad.

80

Si resucitará?

82.

83.

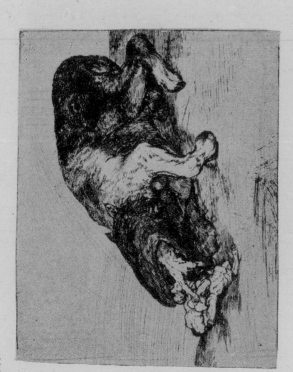

84.

The Art of Bullfighting

(LA TAUROMAQUIA)

The first published series of *The Art of Bullfighting* consisted of thirty-three plates. To this, seven were added in subsequent editions and are doubly designated by numbers and letters. Four more plates rightly belonging to the series are unpublished, rare, and are not available in the United States. These are reproduced in small size from other reproductions. The authentic numbers are found on the upper right corners of the plates.

34 A

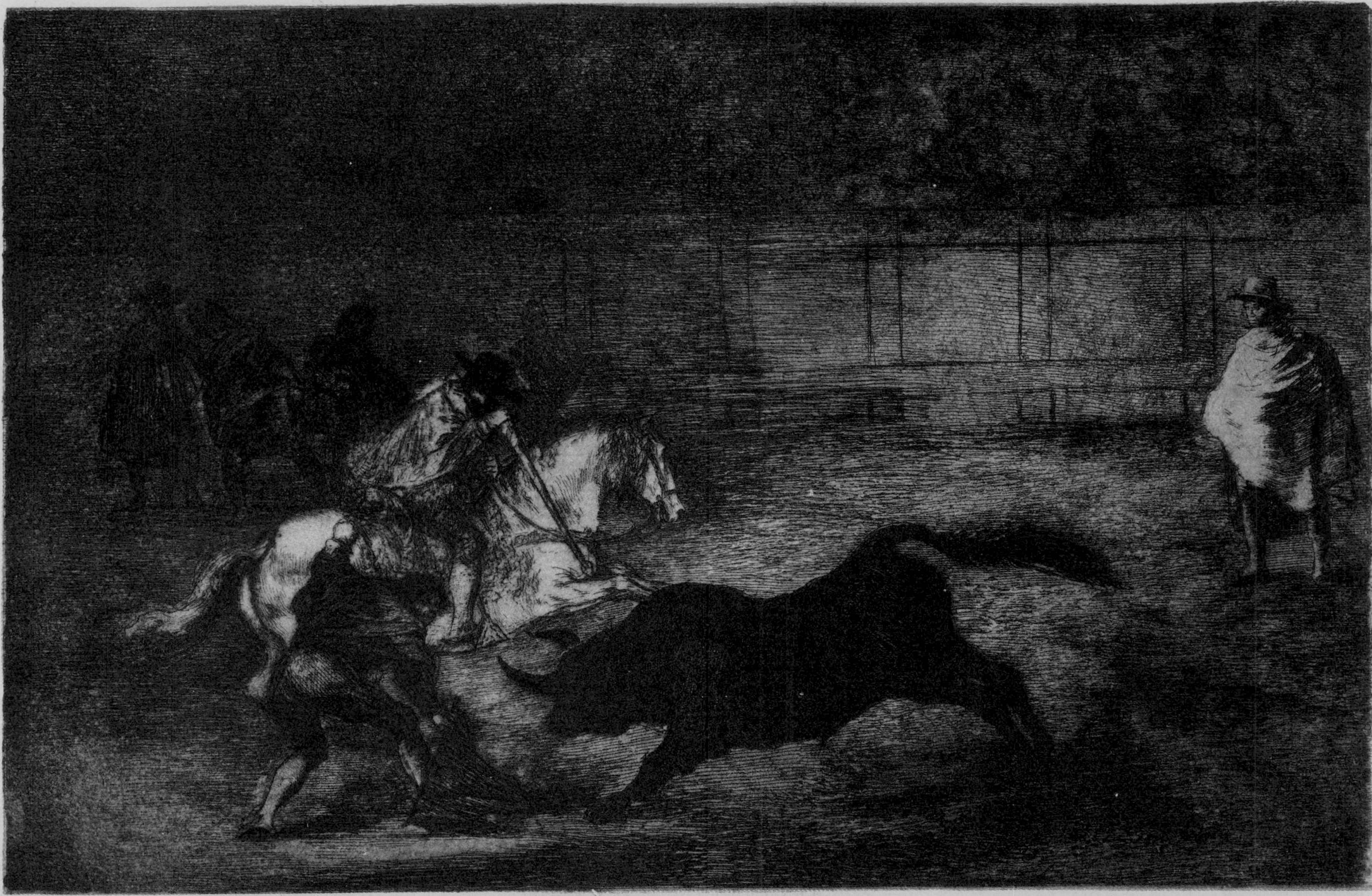

42

44

41

43

The Proverbs

(LOS PROVERBIOS or DISPARATES)

For numbers 8, 10, 12, 16 and 18 there are no Spanish captions. These are therefore translated from the accepted French captions in the catalogue by Loys Delteil. The sequence (numbers at upper right corner of the etchings) is also that of Delteil. The etchings have been presented in variations of this order by many different editors, some of whom have created captions to suit their tastes.

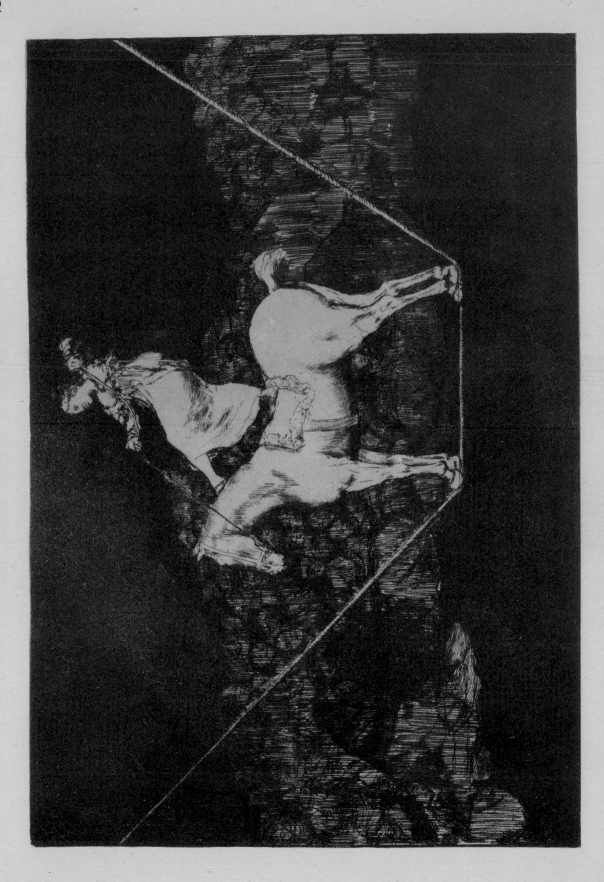

Miscellany

The miscellaneous etchings are not available in originals in this country. As circumstances make it impossible to obtain even photographs of these they are reproduced here, in small size, from other reproductions, chiefly for their reference value. The French captions are those in the Delteil catalogue.

FELIPE III REY DE ESPAÑA.

D. MARGARITA DE AUSTRIA REYNA DE ESPAÑA, MUGER DE PHELIPE III.

FELIPE IV REY DE ESPAÑA.

D. ISABEL DE BORBON REYNA DE ESPAÑA, MUGER DE FELIPE QUARTO.

ÆSOPVS

ESOPO EL FABVLADOR

Pintado p.r D Diego Velazquez y gravado por Franco R. de Nao acabado p.r D Fran.co Goya Pintor a 1778

MOENIPPVS

MENIPO FILOSOFO.

Pintado p.r D.D.on Velazquez y gravado por Franco R. de Nao acabado p.r D. Fran.co Goya Pintor a 1778

D. BALTASAR CARLOS PRINCIPE DE ESPAÑA, HIJO DEL REY D. FELIPE IV. &c.

D.º Gaspar de Guzman, Conde de Olivares, Duque de Sanlucar, &

PINTVRA DE D. DIEGO VELAZQVEZ.
Que Representa á un ENANO y esta en el Palacio R.ˡ de Mad.ᵈ grabada
por D. Fran.ᶜᵒ Goya Pintor el 1778.

Sacada, y grabada del Quadro original, de D. Diego Velazquez, en que representa, al vivo un
Enano del S.ʳ Phelipe IV. por D. Francisco Goya Pintor. Existe en el R.ˡ Palacio de Madrid.
Año de 1778.

37.

38.